Keeping Time Through the Ages

The History of Tools Used to Measure Time

Janey Levy

PowerMath™

The Rosen Publishing Group's
PowerKids Press™
New York

Published in 2004 by The Rosen Publishing Group, Inc.
29 East 21st Street, New York, NY 10010

Copyright © 2004 by The Rosen Publishing Group, Inc.

Book Design: Haley Wilson

Photo Credits: Cover © Huw Jones/Taxi; pp. 4, 27, 28, 29 (digital clock) © PhotoDisc; pp. 6–7 © Gianni
Dagli Orti/Corbis; p. 8 © Adam Woolfitt/Corbis; p. 9 © Paul Almasy/Corbis; pp. 10, 12, 16, 18–19, 25 ©
Bettmann/Corbis; p. 14 © Ed Young/Corbis; p. 20 © Tom Nebbia/Corbis; p. 22 by Janey Levy; p. 24 ©
Michael Boys/Corbis; pp. 26, 30 © Corbis; p. 26 (Galileo) © Hulton/Archive; p. 29 (quartz) © Ross M.
Horowitz/The Image Bank.

Library of Congress Cataloging-in-Publication Data

Levy, Janey.
  Keeping time through the ages : the history of tools used to measure
time / Janey Levy.
       p. cm. — (PowerMath)
Includes index.
Summary: Examines how time has been measured through history, by such
methods as observation of natural cycles and different kinds of clocks
and watches.
  ISBN 0-8239-8993-3 (lib. bdg.)
  ISBN 0-8239-8917-8 (pbk.)
  6-pack ISBN: 0-8239-7444-8
  1. Time measurements—Instruments—Juvenile literature. [1. Time
measurements. 2. Clocks and watches.] I. Title. II. Series.
  QB214.L49 2004
  529'.7—dc21
                                 2002156680

Manufactured in the United States of America

Contents

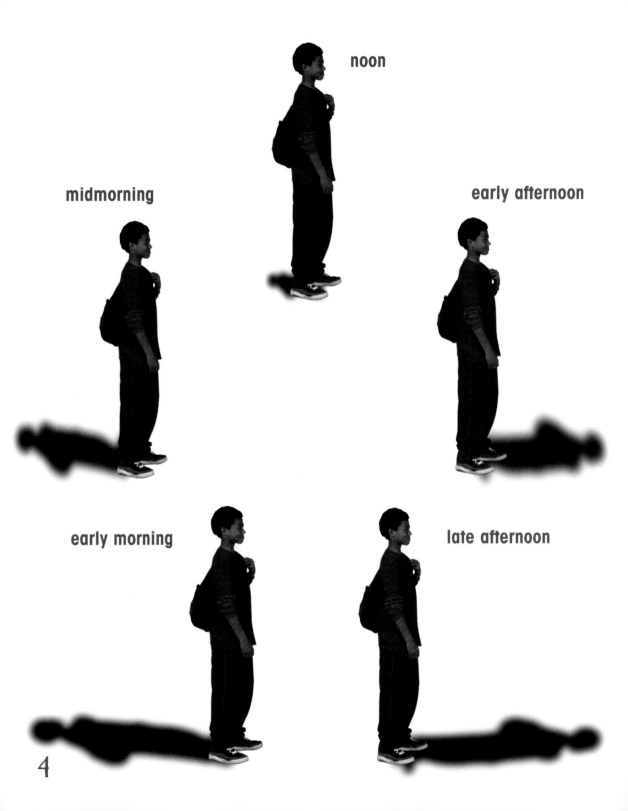

noon

midmorning

early afternoon

early morning

late afternoon

4

Measuring Time with the Sun

Imagine that you live in a world where there are no clocks. How would you know when it is time to get up, go to school, eat lunch, go home, or go to soccer practice? The easiest way to keep track of time would be to use the Sun. That's what people did thousands of years ago.

One of the first things early people observed was that the Sun rose in the east and set in the west. They also noticed that their shadows changed during the day depending on the position of the Sun. Thousands of years ago, people realized they could keep track of time by looking at the length of their shadows. They noticed that early in the day their shadows were very long. Their shadows gradually became shorter as the Sun rose in the sky. At midday, when the Sun was directly overhead, their shadows almost disappeared. Then slowly their shadows grew longer again as the Sun dropped lower in the western sky.

Long ago, people also saw that their shadows pointed in different directions in the morning and afternoon. In the morning, when the Sun is in the east, shadows point toward the west. In the afternoon, when the Sun is in the west, shadows point toward the east.

Around 3500 B.C., ancient Egyptians began to build tall stone structures called **obelisks**. They used the shadows of these obelisks to measure time. They put the obelisks in public places so everyone could use them. At first, Egyptians used the obelisks' shadows just to tell them if it was morning, midday, or afternoon, much as earlier people had used their own shadows.

Later, Egyptians learned to use the way an obelisk's shadow moved during the day to help them measure time in a more **accurate** way. Egyptians put markers in the ground around the obelisk. The movement of the obelisk's shadow from one marker to the next indicated the passing of an hour.

In ancient times, hours were not always of equal length. Egyptians and other early societies divided the time between sunrise and sunset into 12 hours, regardless of whether it was a long summer day or a short winter day. This meant that a summer hour was longer than a winter hour.

Ancient Chinese, Greeks, and Romans also used sundials, as have many other societies throughout history. Sometimes sundials were set up so they were level with the ground; sometimes they were put on walls.

Around 2,000 years later, in 1500 B.C., Egyptians began to make **sundials**. Sundials work the same way as obelisks, but they are much smaller. A sundial is a plate in the shape of a circle or a rectangle that has lines on it to mark the hours. A pointer sticks up from the plate. This pointer casts a shadow on the plate the way an obelisk casts a shadow on the ground.

Obelisks and sundials only worked when there was sunshine. They could not tell time at night or on very cloudy days. People began to look for other ways to measure time. They came up with some amazing inventions.

People even made very small sundials that they could carry with them.

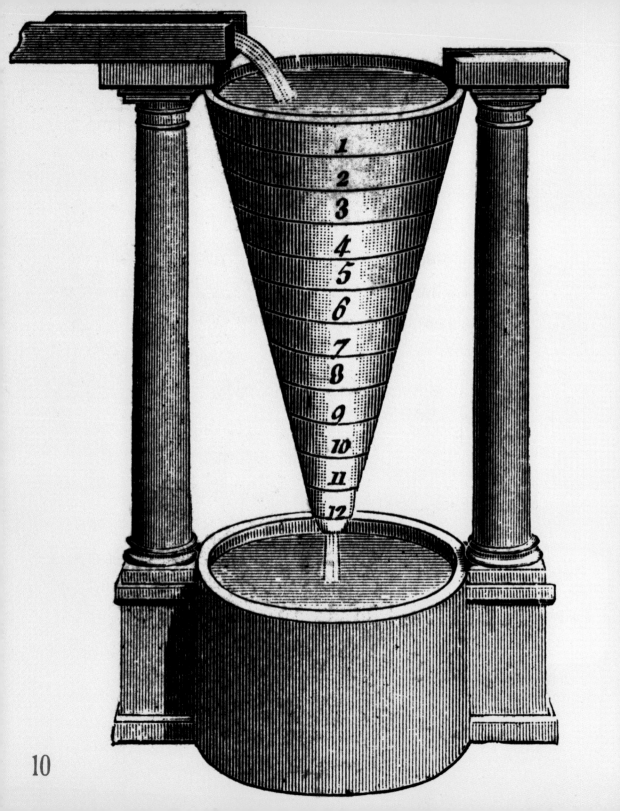

10

Water Clocks and Sand Clocks

Egyptians began to use water clocks around the same time they began to make sundials. One of the oldest water clocks ever found was buried with an Egyptian king, who died around 1500 B.C.

Water clocks were also used by Greeks and Romans, and came in many forms. Some were vessels into which water was poured. These vessels had a hole in the bottom, and time was measured by how much water had dripped out of the vessel. Another kind of water clock was a bowl that was placed in a large container of water. The bowl had a small hole in the bottom, and time was measured by how long it took the bowl to fill with water and sink. The Greeks named the water clock "clepsydra" (KLEP-suh-druh), which means "water thief."

Since water clocks could be used at night and on cloudy days, they were an improvement over sundials. However, early water clocks could not measure the passing of time very accurately. People began to search for ways to make more accurate water clocks.

The sloping sides of this water clock allowed water to drip out of the hole in the bottom at a steady rate. Marks on the vessel measured the passing of hours as the water level in the vessel dropped.

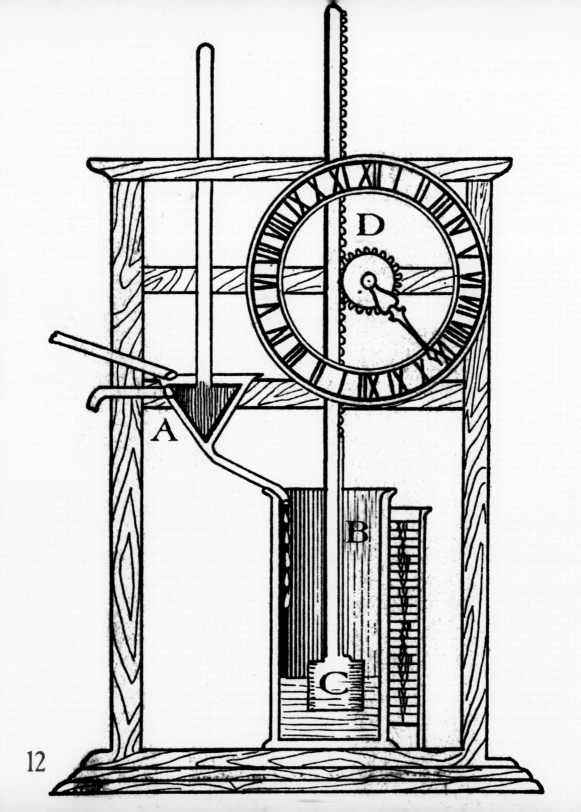

Around 325 B.C., the Greeks found a way to improve the water clock so that it could measure time more exactly. This improved water clock had a face with a hand that moved to point to the hour as the water level changed. This made it much easier to read the time.

Sometime after 100 B.C., a Greek astronomer named Andronikos had a stone clock tower built in the marketplace in the city of Athens. Andronikos's tower showed the time with both sundials and an improved water clock that had a face with a hand to mark the hour. It also displayed the seasons of the year.

Water clocks were also used in ancient China. A famous water clock was built by a Chinese man named Su Sung in 1088 A.D. Su Sung's water clock was a tower that was over 30 feet tall. It had doors that opened to show **mechanical** figures that rang bells and held signs on which the hour was written!

This illustration shows the improved Greek water clock. Water was carried by pipes into the funnel (A). From there it dripped at a steady rate into the tank (B). As the water level in the tank rose, it raised the float (C). The teeth on the rod attached to the float turned the gear (D). The gear moved the hand on the clock face to show the hour.

Another ancient type of clock was the sand clock, also called the sandglass. A sand clock is made of two glass bubbles that are joined by a thin glass neck. The top and bottom are flat so the sand clock can stand on a level surface. Time is measured by how long it takes for the sand to flow from the upper bubble through the thin neck to the lower bubble. Once all the sand is in the lower bubble, the sand clock can be turned over and the process started again.

Sand clocks had some disadvantages. They had to be on flat surfaces to work properly, and sometimes the sand got jammed in the clock's thin neck. However, sand clocks had an important advantage over water clocks—sand didn't freeze in cold weather, as water did.

Sand clocks are sometimes called hourglasses. This name is not really correct, since not all sand clocks measure hours. Some are made to measure times as short as 3 minutes.

King Alfred the Great
of England

16

Candle Clocks and Incense Clocks

People in many different societies learned to use burning candles to measure time. Sometimes a candle was marked with evenly spaced lines. When the burning candle reached one of the lines, it meant an hour had passed. Other candle clocks used candles made of different colored wax. Each layer burned for an hour. Candle clocks were placed inside a vessel to make sure that air currents did not affect how quickly the candle burned.

In the early 1200s, an Arab named al-Jazari improved the candle clock. He made a candle with marbles inside it. The marbles were spaced evenly from the top of the candle to the bottom. When the burning candle reached a marble and melted the wax around it, the marble would fall out. The falling marble dropped on a device that cut the wick and put out the candle's flame. This signaled that an hour had passed.

Candle clocks had some disadvantages. All candles did not burn at the same rate. For instance, fat candles burned more slowly than thin ones did.

King Alfred the Great of England, who lived from 849 A.D. to 899 A.D., used a candle clock to keep track of the hours he worked each day.

In China and Japan, people measured time with **incense** clocks. One type of incense clock used an incense stick laid inside a shallow tray in the shape of an animal, such as a dragon. Pairs of brass beads—each pair connected by a silk thread—were arranged across the open tray so that the beads hung down below the dragon.

The pairs of beads were evenly spaced along the length of the dragon. When the burning incense reached one of the silk threads, it would burn through the thread, causing the beads to drop into a metal dish below. The sound made by the dropping beads signaled the passing of an hour.

In ancient China and Japan, the time between sunrise and sunset was divided into 6 hours. As with the Egyptian system of dividing the daylight time into 12 hours, this meant that a summer hour was longer than a winter hour.

Sometime during the Tang **dynasty**, which lasted from 618 A.D. to 906 A.D., the Chinese invented a special kind of incense clock that actually depended on the sense of smell! A line of powdered incense was sprinkled along a trail in a special vessel. Small amounts of an incense with a different scent, called an "alarm" scent, were placed at fixed points along the trail. When the scent changed, it signaled the passing of an hour.

Incense clocks were used in temples in both China and Japan. The monk who tended the incense clock would strike the temple bell when the alarm scent signaled that an hour had passed. Incense clocks were also used in Japanese teahouses. Teahouses charged people for the amount of time they spent there. When the incense finished burning, a person's time was up.

Incense clocks were often given to a temple by people who worshiped there. The people's names were carved into the clock.

Mechanical Clocks

In the early 1300s, large mechanical clocks began to appear on public buildings in Italy. A mechanical clock was operated by weights inside it that were pulled down by **gravity**. The weights turned a set of wheels and gears, which in turn moved a hand that pointed to the hour on the clock face. By the early 1400s, similar clocks were appearing in cities across Europe. These clocks were often huge and brightly colored, with moving figures that entertained people in the street.

These mechanical clocks measured hours that were the same length in winter as in summer. The idea that all hours should be equal had been introduced in the early 1200s by an Arab named Abu Hassan.

This enormous clock, built around 1400, is on the Town Hall in Prague, Czech Republic. Each hour, the figures on each side of the clock move, two windows above the clock open to show a parade of figures, and a rooster above the windows crows.

23

Around 1500, a German man invented a clock that replaced the weights used in early mechanical clocks with a spring. As the spring inside the clock unwound, it moved the clock's wheels and gears. The clock had to be rewound after the spring finished unwinding.

Since the springs did not unwind at a constant rate, clocks that used springs were not very accurate. However, clocks with springs could be much smaller than clocks that used weights. It became possible to make clocks that could be placed on tables and shelves. People also began to make watches. The watches were 4 or 5 inches wide and about 3 inches thick. That seems huge to us, but at the time people could hardly believe how small the watches were.

Around 1675, a Dutch scientist improved the accuracy of clocks with springs. For the next several centuries, clock makers made fancy clocks for rich people.

Galileo Galilei

Christiaan Huygens

In the late 1500s, an Italian scientist named Galileo Galilei made a discovery that led to more accurate clocks. Galileo discovered that the time it takes a **pendulum** to swing from one side to the other was always the same. In 1656, a Dutch scientist named Christiaan Huygens used Galileo's discovery to make the first successful pendulum clock.

Huygens used a short pendulum, but scientists soon discovered that longer pendulums kept more accurate time. In 1670, an English clock maker made a tall clock with a pendulum that was a yard long. This clock kept more accurate time than any earlier clock had. It was also the first clock to have a minute hand as well as an hour hand.

The English clock used weights to move the gears and used the pendulum to keep the movement steady. The pendulum and weights were put inside a wooden cabinet so they would not be affected by air currents. Today, this type of clock is known as a grandfather clock.

Quartz Clocks and Atomic Clocks

In the 1920s, very accurate clocks were created by using **quartz** crystals. In this kind of clock, a **battery** sends electricity to the crystal, causing it to **vibrate**. This vibration sends out very rapid, evenly spaced electric signals that measure very short amounts of time and control the clock display.

There were some problems with early quartz clocks and watches. The batteries did not last long and had to be replaced often. The quartz crystals were affected by how hot or cold it was, so they ran at different speeds in summer and winter. Those problems have been solved, and today most clocks and watches use quartz crystals.

The vibrations of quartz crystals are also affected by the size and shape of the crystals. Since no two crystals are ever exactly alike, no two quartz clocks or watches ever have exactly the same time.

quartz crystals

In the 1930s, scientists began to look for ways to measure time by using the vibrations of **atoms**. After many experiments, they succeeded in creating an atomic clock that was more accurate than any clock before. Today, official world time is set according to the atomic clock at the National Institute of Science and Technology in Boulder, Colorado.

Scientists in the United States and around the world continue to do experiments, trying to find ways to make clocks that are even more accurate than this atomic clock.

Glossary

accurate (A-kyuh-rut) Able to give facts, such as the correct time, in an exact way.

atom (A-tum) One of the tiny pieces of matter that make up everything in the universe.

battery (BA-tuh-ree) A small electric cell that provides electricity to run a machine.

dynasty (DYE-nuh-stee) A line of rulers from the same family.

gravity (GRA-vuh-tee) The force that pulls objects toward the center of Earth.

incense (IN-sens) Something that burns slowly and gives off a pleasing scent.

mechanical (mih-KA-nih-kul) Operated by a machine.

obelisk (AH-buh-lisk) A tall stone post with four sides that gets narrower as it rises and ends in a point at the top.

pendulum (PEN-juh-lum) A weight at the end of a stick that swings back and forth at a steady rate and controls the movements of a clock.

quartz (KWOHRTS) A crystal rock that vibrates when electricity runs through it.

sundial (SUN-diuhl) An instrument that tells the time of day by the shadow cast on its flat surface by a pointer.

vibrate (VYE-brayt) To move back and forth quickly.

Index